HISTORICAL PERSPECTIVES
In Their Own Words

The Words of
HARRIET TUBMAN

Jagger Youssef

PowerKiDS press™

Published in 2023 by The Rosen Publishing Group, Inc.
2544 Clinton Street, Buffalo, NY 14224

Portions of this work were originally authored by Julia McDonnell and published as *Harriet Tubman in Her Own Words*. All new material in this edition authored by Jagger Youssef.

Editor: Therese Shea
Book Design: Michael Flynn

Photo Credits: Cover https://commons.wikimedia.org/wiki/File:Harriet_Tubman_portrait_photo.jpg; (series background) merrymuuu/Shutterstock.com; (fact box) Miloje/Shutterstock.com; p. 5 https://commons.wikimedia.org/wiki/File:Harriet_Tubman_1895.jpg; p. 7 okili77/Shutterstock.com; p. 9 courtesy of the Library of Congress; pp. 11 (John Brown), 18, 24 Everett Collection/Shutterstock.com; p. 11 (bottom) https://commons.wikimedia.org/wiki/File:Eastman_Johnson_-_A_Ride_for_Liberty_--_The_Fugitive_Slaves_-_Google_Art_Project.jpg; p. 13 https://commons.wikimedia.org/wiki/File:Harriet_Tubman_c1868-69.jpg; p. 14 Library Company of Philadelphia; p. 15 Painters/Alamy Stock Photo; p. 17 https://commons.wikimedia.org/wiki/File:Harriet_Tubman_Reward_Notice_1849.jpg; p. 19 https://commons.wikimedia.org/wiki/File:Undergroundrailroadsmall2.jpg; p. 21 Heidi Besen/Shutterstock.com; p. 23 Zack Frank/Shutterstock.com; p. 25 https://en.wikipedia.org/wiki/Harriet_Tubman#/media/File:Harriet_Tubman_Civil_War_Woodcut.jpg; p. 27 https://commons.wikimedia.org/wiki/File:Harriet_Tubman,_with_rescued_slaves,_New_York_Times.JPG.

Library of Congress Cataloging-in-Publication Data

Names: Youssef, Jagger, author.
Title: The words of Harriet Tubman / Jagger Youssef.
Description: Buffalo, New York : PowerKids Press, [2023] | Series:
    Historical perspectives: in their own words | Includes index.
Identifiers: LCCN 2022028014 (print) | LCCN 2022028015 (ebook) | ISBN
    9781642824629 (library binding) | ISBN 9781642824605 (paperback) | ISBN
    9781642824636 (ebook)
Subjects: LCSH: Tubman, Harriet, 1822-1913--Juvenile literature. |
    Slaves--United States--Biography--Juvenile literature. | African
    American women--Biography--Juvenile literature. | African
    Americans--Biography--Juvenile literature. | Underground
    Railroad--Juvenile literature.
Classification: LCC E444.T82 Y68 2022 (print) | LCC E444.T82 (ebook) |
    DDC 326/.8092 [B]--dc23/eng/20220613
LC record available at https://lccn.loc.gov/2022028014
LC ebook record available at https://lccn.loc.gov/2022028015

Manufactured in the United States of America

CPSIA Compliance Information: Batch #CWPK23. For further information contact Rosen Publishing at 1-800-237-9932.

Find us on 🅕 🅞

CONTENTS

An American Hero.............................4

Born Into Slavery...........................6

A Childhood of Hardship 8

Scarred for Life...........................10

Living in Fear.............................12

Marriage..................................14

Two Escapes...............................16

A Mission.................................18

Greater Danger............................20

Brave and Bold............................22

The Civil War.............................24

A Life of Service.........................26

Glossary..................................30

For More Information......................31

Index.....................................32

AN AMERICAN HERO

When we learn about the beginnings of the United States, we may learn that Native Americans had been in North America thousands of years before Christopher Columbus was born. We may learn about European explorers and settlements. We should also learn that some early Americans didn't come here of their own free will. Instead, they were taken by force from Africa and brought to the Americas as an enslaved workforce.

Slavery was a part of the United States from its founding, but some people fought against it, even helping others escape it. One of the most famous of these freedom fighters was Harriet Tubman. Born into slavery, small in size, and suffering from poor health, Tubman overcame these and other obstacles to become a true American hero.

LOOKING BACK

Sarah Bradford's biographies of Tubman were *Scenes in the Life of Harriet Tubman*, published in 1869, and *Harriet Tubman, Moses of Her People*, published in 1886.

When learning about someone in history, reading their **autobiography**—their words about their own life—is a great way to get to know them. Harriet Tubman never learned to read or write. But an author named Sarah Bradford wrote two biographies of her during her lifetime. Bradford interviewed Tubman and gathered accounts of her deeds. In this book, quotes are presented as closely as possible to those in Bradford's biographies, while making them easier to understand for modern readers.

Tubman's name at birth was Araminta "Minty" Ross. She later took the name "Harriet" after her mother and "Tubman" from her husband.

BORN INTO SLAVERY

Harriet Tubman was born around 1820 in Dorchester County, Maryland. Her grandparents had come from West Africa, enslaved before they even arrived on American soil. Tubman's parents, Benjamin "Old Ben" Ross and Harriet "Rit" Greene, were forced to work for Edward Brodess, whose farm grew corn, rye, and wheat as well as timber.

Tubman spent her early years being cared for by older enslaved women. From a young age, she dreamed of freedom, imagining herself flying over the land and reaching a river. She said, "But it appeared like I wouldn't have the strength [to get across], and just as I was sinking down, there would be ladies . . . and they would put out their arms and pull me 'cross.'"

LOOKING BACK

Harriet Tubman grew up about 100 miles (160 km) from Pennsylvania, a free state.

Those who transported, sold, or bought enslaved people usually didn't care whether they split up parents, children, and brothers and sisters when selling and trading them. But the bonds of the Ross family remained strong despite separation. Harriet Tubman would later rescue her siblings, nieces, nephews, and parents. They communicated in code, snuck food to those who were in hiding, and wore blindfolds so they could say truthfully that they didn't see anyone escape.

MASON-DIXON LINE

The Mason–Dixon Line was the border separating Maryland, Pennsylvania, and Delaware. Before the **American Civil War**, the line, along with the Ohio River, was the boundary between states that allowed enslavement and those that didn't.

A CHILDHOOD OF HARDSHIP

At around five years old, Harriet Tubman began her enslaved life. She ran errands and carried messages, often for distances of several miles. By the time she was six, she was sent to nearby families who paid Edward Brodess for her services, such as weaving, checking animal traps, housekeeping, and caring for babies. She was later a cook and a woodcutter.

These people treated her harshly. As a result, she was often sick and couldn't complete her workload. Sometimes, she was whipped as punishment. Feeling alone, she turned to her faith. She said, "I prayed all the time about my work, everywhere; I was always talking to the Lord." As a teenager, she began to work in the fields as a farm laborer.

LOOKING BACK

Enslavers—the people who thought they owned enslaved men and women—sometimes loaned enslaved people to others in exchange for money, goods, or services.

After she became free, Harriet Tubman hired a lawyer to look into her background. She discovered her mother's enslaver had ordered that her mother should be given to his granddaughter, but receive her freedom when she turned 45 years old. The granddaughter died young, so Harriet's mother was sold instead. Her mother was probably free under the law, but no one ever told her. She and her children—including Harriet—remained enslaved until they escaped.

Children born to enslaved people became enslaved too. Two of Harriet Tubman's sisters were sold and sent away in the 1830s. This photograph shows an enslaved family in South Carolina in 1862.

SCARRED FOR LIFE

Around 1834, Harriet Tubman's life changed. She was in a store when an enslaved man ran in, trying to escape an **overseer**. The overseer caught the freedom seeker and ordered Tubman to hold him while he tied him up. She refused, the man ran, and the overseer threw a heavy lead weight to stop him. It hit Tubman in the head instead, leaving her **unconscious** for days and with a permanent scar. The blow affected her for the rest of her life, causing unexpected sleeping spells, headaches, and visions.

The brutality and inequality of the institution of enslavement became even clearer to Tubman. But her kind nature remained: "I was always praying for poor old master [her enslaver] . . . 'Oh, dear Lord, change that man's heart.'"

A Vision of John Brown

Tubman repeatedly had a dream in which a mob attacked an older bearded man and two younger men. In 1858, after she was free, she met the abolitionist John Brown, who looked like the man in her vision. He tried to begin an uprising against slavery in October 1859. On that day, Tubman had no knowledge of his plan, but insisted she felt a warning about Brown. His two sons were killed,

John Brown was so impressed with Harriet Tubman that he called her "General Tubman."

John Brown

The life of an enslaved person was hard, and being caught escaping could mean terrible beatings or even death. This painting from 1862 shows an enslaved family fleeing by horseback.

LIVING IN FEAR

After she recovered from her injury, Harriet Tubman returned to work. She lived in fear of being sold farther south, so she performed her tasks as well as she could. She preferred to work outside and requested to join her father's lumber-cutting crew. She did such a good job that she was allowed to hire herself out to other families and keep some of the wages she earned.

Though her treatment was slightly better than that of other enslaved people, she still wanted freedom and security: "I grew up like a weed—ignorant of liberty, having no experience of it . . . I was not happy or contented. Every time I saw a white man I was afraid of being carried away. We were always uneasy."

LOOKING BACK

Harriet's father had been freed around 1840. He continued to work on his former enslaver's property, to stay near his family.

Harriet Tubman became known as a strong woman and hard worker. Despite being only 5 feet (1.5 m) tall, she worked as hard as any man. She plowed and planted crops, drove oxen, loaded wagons, and chopped wood. But sometimes those valuable skills brought her unwanted attention. Her enslavers had her perform for guests, hitching her to a boat and loading it with heavy stones. She was made to walk along the riverbank, pulling the boat upstream.

This is a photograph of Harriet Tubman from the late 1860s, after she escaped to freedom.

Around 1844, Harriet married a free Black man named John Tubman. She was still enslaved, however, and any children they had would be enslaved too. A few years later, Harriet became ill and weak. Her enslaver started showing her to other people in order to sell her. She prayed he wouldn't. Her enslaver then died, increasing the chance she'd be sold and separated from her family. She began to think about escaping to the North.

By 1849, Harriet couldn't wait any longer: "I heard that . . . I was to be sent with my brothers in the **chain-gang** to the far South." The fear of being sent away from her family to likely face even harsher punishment than in Maryland prompted her to leave.

enslaved people chained to prevent escape

Harriet had to tell her family and friends she was leaving, but she'd be stopped if the wrong people discovered her plan. So she visited with her friends and family and sang a song that included these lines: "I'm sorry I'm going to leave you" and "I'll meet you in the morning / I'm bound for the Promised Land." Enslaved people often communicated through hymns. Most listeners weren't suspicious.

LOOKING BACK

Between the time she got married and escaped to freedom, she took the name "Harriet" after her mother.

In this painting, first sketched in 1853, enslaved people wait to be sold.

TWO ESCAPES

Tubman and two of her brothers ran away in September 1849, but her brothers decided to turn back. She returned with them. A month later, she tried again, on her own. She left after her husband, who didn't want to go with her, fell asleep. She had heard that a woman in nearby Bucktown would help her, so she knocked on her door. The woman gave her instructions on where to go next.

With the help of the Underground Railroad, Harriet Tubman passed through Maryland and Delaware, hiding in wagons or in plain sight. She eventually reached Pennsylvania. She said, "I looked at my hands to see if I was the same person now I was free. There was such a glory over everything . . . I felt like I was in Heaven."

LOOKING BACK

Freedom seekers risked great dangers: hunting dogs, armed slave-catchers, wild animals, bad weather, and betrayals by their own friends and family.

A Railroad Without Trains

The Underground Railroad wasn't a railroad at all but an organized network of people committed to helping enslaved people reach freedom. It used similar terms as the railroad, though. A "station" or "junction" was a safe place in which to hide. People involved were known as "agents," "conductors," or "station masters." The freedom seekers were "passengers" or "parcels." It had "lines" that traveled through Ohio, Indiana, Pennsylvania, New Jersey, and other states.

THREE HUNDRED DOLLARS REWARD.

RANAWAY from the subscriber on Monday the 17th ult., three negroes, named as follows: HARRY, aged about 19 years, has on one side of his neck a wen, just under the ear, he is of a dark chestnut color, about 5 feet 8 or 9 inches hight; BEN, aged aged about 25 years, is very quick to speak when spoken to, he is of a chestnut color, about six feet high; MINTY, aged about 27 years, is of a chestnut color, fine looking, and about 5 feet high. One hundred dollars reward will be given for each of the above named negroes, if taken out of the State, and $50 each if taken in the State. They must be lodged in Baltimore, Easton or Cambridge Jail, in Maryland.

ELIZA ANN BRODESS.

Near Bucktown, Dorchester county, Md.

Oct. 3d, 1849.

please copy office.

This is a notice in a newspaper offering a reward for "Minty" (Harriet's nickname) after she had run away.

Tubman traveled to Philadelphia, Pennsylvania, where she found jobs to earn money. But she was lonely without her family. She became involved in antislavery groups like the Vigilance Committee, which provided runaways with food and shelter. Soon, she was given the opportunity to guide people to freedom. A man asked for help rescuing a woman and her children from Maryland. Tubman listened to his story and realized he was talking about her own family. She insisted on taking the mission, later saying, "My home, after all, was down in the old cabin quarter [in Maryland], with the old folks, and my brothers and sisters . . . They should be free also."

Once the Underground Railroad brought her family to Baltimore, Tubman led them into Pennsylvania and freedom. Many other trips followed.

Underground Railroad agents help enslaved people seeking freedom

Abolishing the Evil

Abolitionists were people who worked to end the institution of enslavement. They organized themselves into a movement around 1830. They published newspapers, gave speeches, and tried to get laws passed making slavery illegal. Many people joined the cause, despite the dangers. Abolitionist William Lloyd Garrison was almost killed by an angry mob because of his writings. Abolitionists included whites, Blacks, men, and women.

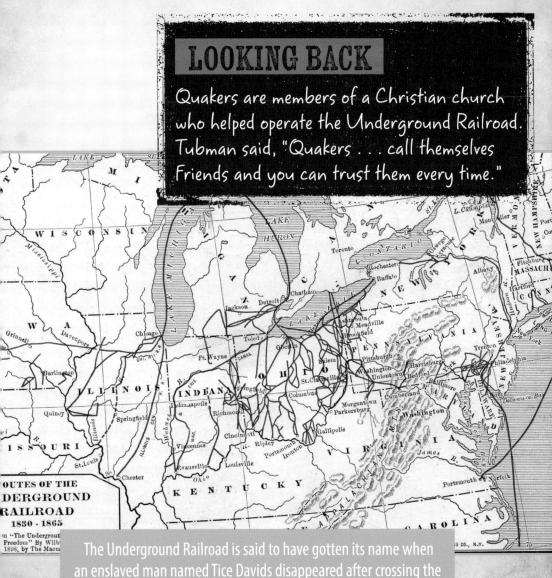

LOOKING BACK

Quakers are members of a Christian church who helped operate the Underground Railroad. Tubman said, "Quakers . . . call themselves Friends and you can trust them every time."

OUTES OF THE
DERGROUND
RAILROAD
1830 - 1865

m "The Undergrou
Freedom" By Wilb
1898, by The Macm

The Underground Railroad is said to have gotten its name when an enslaved man named Tice Davids disappeared after crossing the Ohio River. "He must have gone on an underground road," someone said. This map shows routes of the Underground Railroad.

GREATER DANGER

In 1850, the Fugitive Slave Act became law. It required all parts of the United States, even states that had outlawed enslavement, to take part in returning enslaved people who ran away. So Harriet Tubman changed the destination of her journeys. "I wouldn't trust Uncle Sam with my people . . . I brought 'em all clear off to Canada," she said. She used a route 650 miles (1,046 km) long between Maryland and the Canadian city of St. Catharines.

Tubman worked as a cook and housekeeper in New Jersey during the summer to fund the trips she made, guiding freedom seekers along the Underground Railroad. When she reflected on her many successful rescues, she remarked, "I can say what most conductors can't say—I never ran my train off the track and I never lost a passenger."

LOOKING BACK

Harriet Tubman was finally able to lead her parents to freedom in Canada in 1857.

A New Moses

Tubman earned a new nickname—"Moses." Moses was the Bible figure who led his people out of slavery in Egypt. Freedom seekers in Tubman's time compared their forbidden journey—sometimes several weeks long—through unfamiliar and dangerous territory toward a "promised land" in the North to the journey the **Israelites** took thousands of years before. Soon whites and Blacks, Northerners and Southerners, were using the name Moses for Tubman too.

This statue of Harriet Tubman leading people to the North is in Boston, Massachusetts.

BRAVE AND BOLD

Harriet Tubman bought a house in Auburn, New York, in 1859. Her parents moved from Canada to live with her. She began giving passionate antislavery speeches, drawing large audiences. She was still willing to undertake dangerous missions too.

In 1860, an escaped enslaved man named Charles Nalle was caught in Troy, New York. Tubman led a crowd that grabbed him from his guards. Shielding him with her own body, she cried, "Drag us out! Drag him to the river! Drown him! But don't let them have him!"

Two men were shot in the struggle, but Nalle was smuggled into Canada in a wagon. Tubman went into hiding. She became convinced that slavery couldn't be ended without violence: "They may say, 'Peace, Peace' . . . I know it's going to be war."

LOOKING BACK

Another of Tubman's tricks was to plan escapes on Saturday nights. Sunday was a day of no work, so missing workers likely wouldn't be noticed until Monday.

Tubman was clever as well as brave. While at a railroad station in the South, she saw a poster with her picture offering a reward for her capture. She heard two men arguing whether she was the person in the poster. She opened a book she was carrying and fooled them into thinking she was reading. Since people knew Tubman couldn't read, they thought she wasn't Harriet Tubman.

Harriet Tubman's home and the property around it in Auburn, New York, is now a national historic park.

Harriet Tubman was correct in believing that a war would break out in the United States. The American Civil War between the Northern states and the Southern states began in 1861. She was asked to help the many enslaved people who were abandoned in the South and left hungry and homeless. She also served as a nurse to **Union** soldiers and led bands of Black troops on scouting missions.

Tubman found herself close to battle: "We saw the lightning, and that was the guns; and then we heard thunder, and that was the big guns; and then we heard the rain falling, and that was drops of blood falling, and when we came to get in the crops, it was dead men that we reaped."

Another Fearless Feat

Tubman was the only woman to plan and lead a military operation during the American Civil War. Under her guidance, three Union gunboats manned by Black soldiers traveled down South Carolina's Combahee River, burning farms and gathering supplies. Local enslaved people raced to the riverbank and boarded the vessels. **Confederate** forces were caught off guard. It was an overwhelming victory for the North, and over 700 enslaved people were freed.

LOOKING BACK

Around 1863, Tubman worked as spy for the Union, using information gathered by enslaved people to report on the movements of Confederate forces.

This is a **woodcut** of Harriet Tubman as she looked during the Civil War.

A LIFE OF SERVICE

Harriet Tubman returned to her home in Auburn after the war was over. Slavery was ended, but many people were left in need. She shared what little money she had. She still had the energy and drive to support her causes, which included women's **suffrage** and education for Black children. She also founded a home for the needy, sick, and poor. Tubman moved into that facility, the Harriet Tubman Home, in 1911 and stayed until her death on March 10, 1913.

Tubman's work had achieved liberty for herself and countless others. Social reformer Gerrit Smith wrote of her, "Nearly all the nation over, [Harriet Tubman] has been heard of for her wisdom, integrity, patriotism, and bravery. The cause of freedom owes her much. The country owes her much."

LOOKING BACK

Tubman married Nelson Davis in 1869. They adopted a daughter named Gertie in 1874.

Thomas Garrett, an Underground Railroad conductor, said, "I never met with any person, of any color, who had more confidence in the voice of God." Tubman believed visions she experienced carried **divine** messages and was sure her prayers were heard. She didn't take credit for her deeds, saying, "It wasn't me; 'twas the Lord! Just so long as he wanted to use me, he would take care of me . . . I always told him, 'I'm going to hold steady onto you, and you've got to see me through.'"

This photo from 1887 shows Tubman (far left), her daughter Gertie (second from left), and her husband Nelson Davis (seated, third from left). The other people shown are neighbors and people staying at Tubman's home.

Historians still **debate** the number of enslaved people Harriet Tubman saved. About 70 people and 13 trips to the South are **confirmed**. She may have instructed around 70 more people about how they could make the journey on their own. But numbers don't reflect the true depth of her life. Born into enslavement, she won her own freedom and went on to assume remarkable roles: Underground Railroad conductor, abolitionist, nurse, spy, suffragist, and caregiver to the poor and needy.

The United States today honors Harriet Tubman with schools in her name and statues in her image. Service organizations for the needy continue the efforts she began later in life, which she called her "last work." She was also the first Black woman honored with a U.S. stamp. Her life continues to be admired today.

LOOKING BACK

In 2021, the U.S. government announced it was planning to place Tubman's image on the $20 bill.

Tubman used her mind—and her persistence—to accomplish difficult goals. When she needed money to establish a home for elderly and disabled Black Americans, she asked for contributions. She visited a certain man to ask him for $20. She had said, "I ain't going to leave there, and I ain't going to eat or drink, till I get money enough." At first, the man refused. So Tubman sat there all day long—and eventually raised $60.

Timeline of Harriet Tubman's Life

1820 — Araminta "Minty" Ross is born in Dorchester County, Maryland.

1834 — She suffers a head injury that has lifelong effects.

1844 — She marries John Tubman and takes his last name and the first name "Harriet."

1849 — She travels to Pennsylvania to escape slavery.

1850 — She makes the first of many trips to rescue other enslaved people.

1857 — She helps her parents escape from slavery and settles in Auburn, New York.

1858 — She meets abolitionist John Brown.

1860 — She rescues Charles Nalle.

1862 — She begins to serve as a nurse, scout, and spy for Union forces during the Civil War.

1869 — She marries Nelson Davis.

1908 — She opens the Harriet Tubman Home for the Aged for Black Americans in need.

1913 — She dies in Auburn, New York, and is buried with military honors.

GLOSSARY

American Civil War: A war fought from 1861 to 1865 between the North and the South in the United States over slavery and other issues.

autobiography: A book that tells the story of a person's life that is written by the person it is about.

chain-gang: A group of prisoners chained together, often to do some kind of work.

Confederate: Having to do with the Confederate States of America, made up of the Southern states that left the United States between 1860 and 1865.

confirm: To find to be true.

debate: To formally discuss or argue.

divine: Relating to, or coming from, a god.

Israelite: A person who lived in the ancient northern kingdom of Israel.

overseer: A boss or supervisor.

suffrage: The right to vote.

unconscious: Unable to see, hear, or sense what is happening because of accident or injury.

Union: Having to do with the group of states that remained part of the United States after Southern states separated in 1860 and 1861 and formed the Confederacy.

woodcut: A print that is designed on a block of wood.

FOR MORE INFORMATION

Books

Buckley, Jr., James. *Harriet Tubman: Fighter for Freedom!* San Diego, CA: Printers Row Publishing Group, 2020.

Jazynka, Kitson. *Harriet Tubman.* New York, NY: DK Publishing, 2019.

Kramer, Barbara. *Harriet Tubman.* Washington, D.C.: National Geographic, 2020.

Websites

Harriet Tubman's Auburn Home
www.nps.gov/hart/learn/historyculture/tubman-residence.htm
See where Tubman spent her life after she found freedom.

Harriet Tubman Historical Society
www.harriet-tubman.org/
This site offers much more information about her life and achievements.

The Underground Railroad
www.pbs.org/wgbh/aia/part4/4p2944.html
Read more about the life-saving work of the Underground Railroad.

INDEX

A
abolitionists, 10, 19, 28, 29
American Civil War, 7, 24, 25, 26, 29
Auburn, New York, 22, 23, 26, 29

B
birth, 4, 5, 6, 29
Bradford, Sarah, 4, 5
Brodess, Edward, 6, 8
brothers, 7, 14, 16, 18
Brown, John, 10, 11, 29

C
Canada, 20, 22

D
Davis, Gertie, 26, 27
Davis, Nelson, 26, 27, 29
death, 26, 29

F
Fugitive Slave Act, 22

G
grandparents, 6

H
Harriet Tubman Home for the Aged, 26, 29

N
Nalle, Charles, 22, 29
name, 5, 15, 29

P
parents, 6, 7, 9, 12, 14, 15, 20, 22, 29

S
sisters, 7, 9, 18

T
Tubman, John, 5, 14, 16, 29

U
Underground Railroad, 16, 17, 18, 19, 20, 27, 28